Instant Node Package Manager

Create your own node modules and publish them on
npm registry, automating repetitive tasks in between

Juzer Ali

BIRMINGHAM - MUMBAI

Instant Node Package Manager

First published: September 2013

Second Published: October 2013

Production Reference: 2031013

Published by Packt Publishing Ltd.
Livery Place
35 Livery Street
Birmingham B3 2PB, UK.

ISBN 978-1-78328-333-0

www.packtpub.com

Credits

Author

Juzer Ali

Reviewer

Tim Oxley

Acquisition Editor

Owen Roberts

Commissioning Editor

Subho Gupta

Technical Editors

Tanvi Bhatt

Akashdeep Kundu

Project Coordinator

Akash Poojary

Proofreader

Lucy Rowland

Production Coordinator

Prachali Bhiwandkar

Cover Work

Prachali Bhiwandkar

Cover Image

Ronak Dhruv

About the Author

Juzer Ali was born and brought up in a small Indian town of Mhow near Indore, Madhya Pradesh. After finishing school in Mhow he took up an Electronics and Telecommunication Engineering course at Devi Ahilya Vishwa Vidyalaya, Indore. During his college days, irrespective of his branch of study, he was always interested in learning computer programming.

After graduating he worked for two and a half years at Tata Consultancy Services (TCS) as a full stack engineer. It was during this tenure that Juzer came across node.js technology and started exploring it. Juzer has made some open source contributions and is a co-maintainer of node-elasticsearch-client project and the author of crawl.js and expressive-router node modules. He tried to spread JavaScript best practices and evangelize node.js at TCS. Currently he is working as a node.js consultant with a multinational company.

Although he was inclined towards writing since childhood, he never undertook serious writing on a technical subject before this book. He has been writing short fiction stories on his blog since adolescence.

Acknowledgement

A book never belongs to a single person. For this short crisp book, there were more than a dozen people responsible and each person's contribution was critical for its completion. First of all I am grateful to my family; my parents, my fiancée Fatema, and my brother and friend Yusuf for constantly believing in me and in many aspects of my life. Because of this I was able to undertake and execute this project confidently. My nieces Zainab, Tasneem, and little Sakina are the apples of my eye and remain major sources of inspiration to me.

I am ever so thankful to Ankit Jain for his critical reviews, which stood in my way of submitting a poorly structured draft. Harendra and Sahil's constant encouragement and deep interest in the progress of this book kept me going when things were rough. I want to extend this gratitude to Nikhar, Udit, Priyank, Mohit, Mayur, and all those friends and family members who shared my joy and pleasure in writing this book. Each little pat on the back meant a lot to me.

My seniors at Tata Consultancy Services, Nikunj and Niraj's contributions were also instrumental in that they constantly reinforced beliefs in my technical understanding and permitted me to concentrate on this book more than the chores at work during my last few days at TCS.

Lastly, I am thankful to Packt Publishing crew, especially Priyanka and Akash who suggested to me the idea of writing this book and gave me a chance to contribute to the growing node. js community with this humble effort. Their contributions were significant in managing the schedule and the process of exchanging and correcting the drafts. This wouldn't have been possible without their efforts.

There might have been more people behind the scenes who have contributed to this book in more subtle ways. I want to thank them all for putting effort into this book.

About the Reviewer

Tim Oxley is currently working for an Australian node.js-powered hardware company, Ninja Blocks. He runs the SingaporeJS meetup and Australian JavaScript conference. He was an enterprise Flex developer and is now an open source Flex developer. He also works as a node.js freelancer.

www.PacktPub.com

Support files, eBooks, discount offers and more

You might want to visit www.PacktPub.com for support files and downloads related to your book.

Did you know that Packt offers eBook versions of every book published, with PDF and ePub files available? You can upgrade to the eBook version at www.PacktPub.com and as a print book customer, you are entitled to a discount on the eBook copy. Get in touch with us at service@packtpub.com for more details.

At www.PacktPub.com, you can also read a collection of free technical articles, sign up for a range of free newsletters and receive exclusive discounts and offers on Packt books and eBooks.

PacktLib.PacktPub.com

Do you need instant solutions to your IT questions? PacktLib is Packt's online digital book library. Here, you can access, read and search across Packt's entire library of books.

Why Subscribe?

- ✦ Fully searchable across every book published by Packt
- ✦ Copy and paste, print and bookmark content
- ✦ On demand and accessible via web browser

Free Access for Packt account holders

If you have an account with Packt at www.PacktPub.com, you can use this to access PacktLib today and view nine entirely free books. Simply use your login credentials for immediate access.

Table of Contents

Instant Node Package Manager

Welcome to *Instant Node Package Manager*. This book has been specially created to provide you with all the information that you need to get set up with node.js and npm. You will learn the basic usage of node package manager, get started with building your first node module, and discover some tips and tricks for using the npm command line.

This document contains the following sections:

So, what is Node Package Manager? describes what npm actually is, what you can do with it, and why it's so great.

Installation helps us to learn how to download and install node.js and npm with minimum fuss, and then set it up so that you can use it as soon as possible.

Quick start – creating your first npm module will show you how to perform one of the core tasks of npm: creating and installing node modules with a simple yet powerful example. Follow the steps to create your own node module, and automate installing and publishing the modules, and publish your node module on standard npm registry.

Top 10 features you need to know about will help you to learn how to perform 10 tasks with the most important features of npm. By the end of this section you will be able to install dependencies on external node modules automatically, resolve dependencies by linking locally, publish your code on standard npm registry, create and publish node.js executables, and running arbitrary scripts on certain events.

People and places you should get to know shows that every open source project is centered on a community. This section provides you with many useful links to the project page and forums, as well as a number of helpful articles, tutorials, blogs, and the Twitter feeds of node.js super-contributors.

So, what is Node Package Manager?

We have always known JavaScript as the language of the web. It is dynamically typed, implemented in C++ by most browsers, and provides API to interact with a web page. A simplistic way to describe node.js would be JavaScript that runs on the server-side. But that would be an understatement. node.js takes the JavaScript implementation to another level by augmenting it so that it can do pretty much everything that a server-side technology should be capable of doing. node.js can be used to:

+ Start an http/https server
+ Make http/https requests to other web servers
+ Start the TCP/UDP server or to make TCP/UDP requests
+ Read and write content on the filesystem
+ Spawn and manage new processes on operating system

The runtime of node.js is powered by Google's V8 JavaScript engine, whose task is to compile and run JavaScript code. V8 is the same engine that powers Google Chrome's JavaScript runtime.

The feature that separates node.js from other platforms is what is known as evented I/O. In node.js, during an I/O operation, whenever a chunk of data is read or written, an event is emitted. The programmer needs to register callbacks to react to these events, for example, to aggregate the chunks being read, or to determine whether the operation has been completed. This allows for making the I/O operations asynchronous, thus saving CPU cycles from being wasted. Other platforms make use of CPU time during I/O operations through multithreading. But an event-driven approach is much more efficient, because there is no thread spawning overhead and the memory footprint is much smaller.

To assist the evented I/O model, node.js has an event loop, which is constantly asking if there are there any more events to process. Whenever an event occurs, it gets registered into an event queue. The event loop executes the event handlers in the queue one by one. If there are no more events to process, the node.js runtime exits; of course, that is not true if you have started a server, in that case it will wait for events to occur.

To translate I/O operation into events, node.js uses `libuv`. `libuv` is a C++ library that provides infrastructure for evented I/O. The actual magic happens in the libraries written on top of `libuv`, node.js itself is just a thin JavaScript wrapper around these. Nonetheless, node.js is an excellent platform for writing programs involving large amount of I/O operations that scales really well.

Every mature platform has to face problems of modularization and redistribution of code. This is exactly the problem that Maven solved for Java, or the problem that **Gems** solved for **Ruby**, and thus npm for node.js.

We want to write JavaScript libraries and we want to be able to pass those libraries around. Anyone who wants to use those libraries, or what are being referred to as packages or node modules, should be able to install them with minimum number of steps possible. That is where **node package manager (npm)** comes in.

npm allows us to register our packages with a name so that we can import/export these packages using the registered name. Moreover, npm also integrates with the npm registry. The npm registry is a web service that hosts such packages. The standard npm registry is hosted at `https://npmjs.org`. It is accessible on open internet and is maintained by Joyent, the organization that sponsors node.js development. We can publish our packages on the npm registry, and it can be found on the npm registry website by its name. For example, an author has published his package by the name "express". We can obtain that package by running `npm install express` on our machine or by visiting `http://npmjs.org/package/express`. This way of distributing code over the internet is the reason why npm exists.

Previously, npm required separate installation. Recent versions of node.js ships with npm included.

Now that we know what node.js and npm are, in the next section we shall proceed to installing node.js on a computer.

Installation

In this section, we will get node.js and npm installed and running on our machines. Earlier node.js and npm required separate installations. But in later versions npm made it to the core of node.js, and now comes bundled with it. We will use command line extensively throughout this book, including during installation. npm does not provide any tool with graphical user interface, so some familiarity with the command line is necessary to work with it.

Step 1 – what do I need?

Before beginning to install node.js, you will need to check that your system meets the following requirements:

+ **Disk Space**: 50 MB free (min). This much should suffice for all our needs of installing node.js and creating our own programs. However, as you begin using elaborate node.js packages and libraries, you might need more space to store them.
+ **Memory**: 256 MB (min); 1 GB (recommended).
+ **Operating System**: node.js supports a wide range of operating systems including Windows, Mac, Solaris, and Linux. It is unlikely that you will fail to install node.js due to an operating system.

Step 2 – downloading node.js

Download instructions vary for different platforms. We have provided instructions for three most popular platforms, Windows, Mac, and *nix flavored operating systems. The instructions for Linux hold for most of the derivatives and distributions. You need to download the respective files from node.js downloads page: `http://nodejs.org/download`.

Windows or Mac

The easiest way to install node.js on Windows/Mac is through respective installers.

Step 1 – downloading Windows/MAC installer

Download the Windows installer `.msi` package from the download page (`http://nodejs.org/download`). If you are using Mac, download the Mac `.pkg` instead.

Step 2 – running the installer

Run the installer by double-clicking it and follow the instructions.

Step 3 – testing

Open the Windows command prompt or a terminal on Mac OS and provide the following instructions:

```
$ node --version
v0.10.5
$ npm --version
1.2.10
```

Linux and other Unices

There are lots of ways of installing node on *nix flavored Operating Systems. The instructions given here will hold for most of them.

One step installation

There is a one-step installation process by which you can install node.js through command line. But that may not always work.

```
$ echo prefix = ~/local >> ~/.npmrc
$ sudo curl https://npmjs.org/install.sh | sh
```

Foolproof installation

Following is a step-by-step guide for manual installation.

Step 1 – getting the binary

Go to `http://nodejs.org/download/` and choose Linux Binaries. Choose a 32-bit or a 64-bit version according to your machine's CPU architecture. If you don't know what this means, choose 32-bit. A `tar.gz` file will be downloaded with a name similar to `node-v0.10.5-linux-x86.tar.gz`. The file name might differ depending upon the version of node, operating system, and your computer architecture. In general, the name will follow the pattern, node-v<version>-<OS>-<architecture>`.tar.gz`.

 If you are using **Solaris (SunOS)** download SunOS binaries instead.

Step 2 – extracting the file

Extract the file either using your favorite GUI based extractor or using command line.

```
$ cd path/to/downloaded/tar-file
$ tar -xvf  node-v0.10.5-linux-x86.tar.gz
```

You should be left with a folder named `node-v0.10.5-linux-x86`.

Step 3 – testing

```
$ cd  node-v0.10.5-linux-x86/bin
$ ./node --version && ./npm --version
```

This should print something like the following:

```
v0.10.5
1.2.10
```

Step 4 – symlink

Binaries are runnable pieces of code that can be directly run from the command line. This package has given us exactly that. But to run them, we need to locate them on our machine. We don't want to remember where we have stored the binaries. That's why we will put them in a location which is present in our system's PATH variable so that they can be accessed from anywhere. To do that, we will symlink the binaries to: /usr/local/sbin.

```
$ sudo ln -s ./node /usr/local/sbin/node
$ sudo ln -s ./npm /usr/local/sbin/npm
```

If you do not have super user privilege on your machine you can add the node.js binary folder on your system's PATH variable instead:

```
$ export PATH=PATH:/path/to/nodejsfolder/node-v0.10.5-linux-x86/bin
```

Step 5 – testing symlink

```
$ cd to/a/random/location/on/your/computer
$ node --version && npm --version
v0.10.5
1.2.10
```

Various Linux distributions provide node.js from their package distributions. You can install node.js from your respective package distribution. Specific instructions for most distros can be found at https://github.com/joyent/node/wiki/Installing-Node.js-via-package-manager. Usually these distros do not keep up with the node.js development and are several versions old.

Installing via nvm and nave (recommended)

On *nix systems, installing node directly as binaries doesn't help much in keeping the installation up to date. In fact, you will have to repeat the exact instructions again for the version you want to upgrade or downgrade to. **node version manager** (**nvm**) is a shell program that provides a convenient way of trying multiple node.js versions at the same time.

Switching between two versions is just a matter of running one shell command. It does this by creating a virtual environment. What this means is that nvm keeps binaries in a user's home directory. Whenever the user instructs it to change versions, nvm manipulates the system's PATH variable so that it exposes the binary requested.

Github URL for nvm is `https://github.com/creationix/nvm.git` where you can find the instructions for installing and using nvm. In a nutshell, following sequence of instructions will install node v0.10.

```
wget -qO- https://raw.github.com/creationix/nvm/master/install.sh | sh
source ~/.nvm/nvm.sh # do it every time a new shell is started
nvm install 0.10
nvm use 0.10
```

You can install different versions of node by using `nvm install` command and switch between these versions by using `nvm use` command. Note that the second command, `source ~/.nvm/.nvm.sh` has to be run every time a new shell is started. To automate this step, add the command at the end of `~/.bashrc file`.

A similar program called nave also exists which accomplishes the same purpose. It can be found at `https://github.com/isaacs/nave`. Nave also creates a virtual environment for testing out different versions of node. There are subtle differences between nvm and nave, the major one being that nvm downloads binaries directly, while nave compiles each version from source. Nave requires you to have a C++ compiler installed on your system.

You can go through the README of both the programs and choose for yourself the one that fits your needs. Generally any one of them should work for most purposes.

Installing node through nave or nvm is recommended since it will help you test your modules between different versions quickly.

The downside of using virtual environment is that it will be available only for the user who has installed it and not other users on the same system.

Building and installing from source

If you are interested in building and installing node.js from its source code, the detailed instructions are available on the wiki of node.js github repository. Here is the link: `https://github.com/joyent/node/wiki/Installation`.

And that's it!

We are now ready to explore node.js and build our very first module.

Quick start – creating your first npm module

In this chapter we will code some JavaScript and we will learn techniques to reuse the code in different files and modules. We will also create our first node module and then publish it on the standard npm registry.

simplemath library

During the course of this section we will try to create a node module named `simplemath`. It will be a simple library. We won't delve much into programming paradigm in node.js, or nuances of JavaScript. Our library will simply provide basic operations like addition, subtraction, multiplication, division, and a few convenient constants. Through building this module we will learn how to use npm to create and publish node modules. We will follow the test-driven development strategy to build this library. We will write failing tests before starting to code our application and then try to pass those tests.

Step 1 – learning to use require()

To begin with consider the `sum` function from our `simplemath` library:

```
function sum(num1, num2) {
    return num1 + num2;
}
```

This is a simple JavaScript program. It is a function which expects two integer arguments and returns the sum of the two numbers. To make this function available to other files and programs, we will have to add only a single line of code on top of the file. So the code looks like the following code listing:

```
module.exports = sum;

function sum(num1, num2) {
  return num1 + num2;
}
```

The `module.exports` object has a very special meaning in node.js. We can assign any entity to it, and we will be able to access that entity from outside that file. Let's try it out in node.js REPL. For those who don't know, a **REPL (Read Eval Print Loop)** is an interactive command-line program that one can use to try out the language features. We can enter node.js REPL by entering `node` on the command line.

```
$ node
> var someVar = require('./sum.js');
> someVar;
[Function: sum]
```

After we arrive at node (>) prompt we call `require()` with path of the file `sum.js` as argument and attached the returned value to a variable named `someVar`. On inspecting the `someVar` variable we come to know that it is a function named `sum`. Let's find out what `toString()` of `someVar` gives us:

```
> someVar.toString();
'function sum(num1, num2) {\n\t\treturn num1 + num2;\n}'
```

This is actually the complete body of the `sum` function that we've defined in our file. Finally, when we call the function with appropriate arguments:

```
> someVar(1,2)
3
```

What actually happened is that the function that we had assigned to `module.exports` in our `sum.js` file, got returned by the `require('./sum.js')` call and was assigned to `someVar`. Behind the scenes, the JavaScript code in `sum.js` is run immediately on calling `require`. Keep in mind though that the function itself isn't called but just returned. We will have to call the function to run the code inside that. Anything that we assigned to `module.exports` is returned by the `require` call.

One caveat to keep in mind is that assignment to `module.exports` has to be done immediately and not asynchronously. So for example, although the following code works:

```
(function(){
   module.exports = {"key": "value"};
})();
```

The following doesn't:

```
setTimeout(function(){
   module.exports = {"key": "value"};
   }, 0);
```

So that was using `require` from command line. Note the action performed by `require` is similar to that of `import` in programming languages such as python and Java. It gives access to code written in a file to somewhere outside the file. Now let's use `require` in another file that contains node.js code.

```
var sum = require("./sum");
console.log( sum(1,2) );
```

The preceding code again loads the `sum.js` file (the `.js` extension is optional, and as we will see, so is `.node` and `.json`) and prints the result of calling `sum(1,2)` on standard output. Save the preceding code in another file. Name it `tests.js` and keep it in the same directory as `sum.js`. Let's run `tests.js` from command line.

```
$ node tests.js
3
```

Thus, we have successfully used code from one file into another.

Using `require` is not limited to importing functions. We can import any JavaScript entity, including but not limited to strings, numbers, and objects. The `require` function also supports importing a `.json` file (a file whose body is JSON). For example, we can have following two files:

foo.js

```
module.exports = { "foo": "bar"};
```

foo.json

```
{ "foo": "bar" }
```

Calling `require` with ./`foo.js` and ./`foo.json` will be equivalent and it will load a JavaScript object with a key named `foo` and its value equal to `bar`. The filename that we pass to `require` should be a valid file name with path. So we can also pass paths which are outside the directory like `require("../filename")`. From node.js documentation (`http://nodejs.org/api/modules.html`):

> *If the exact filename is not found, then node will attempt to load the required filename with the added extension of* `.js`, `.json`, *and then* `.node`. `.js` *files are interpreted as JavaScript text files, and* `.json` *files are parsed as* JSON *text files.*
>
> *A module prefixed with / is an absolute path to the file. For example,* `require('/home/marco/foo.js')` *will load the file at* /home/marco/foo.js.

Another use of `require` is to load the core modules or native modules. Core modules are modules that are baked into the source code of node.js. They are the APIs that we talked about in the first section or rather the APIs that constitute node.js itself. For example, following code will load the http module from node.js core:

```
var http = require("http");
```

Note that there is no leading slash or dot for loading a core module or any external module for that matter. It's also worth noting that if the namespace of two modules clashes, that is, if two modules have the same name, the core module will always trump the external module.

Native modules

What we can do with node.js is limited to what is already implemented in underlying meta language, which is C++ in our case. The current version of node.js provides a wide range of implementations of general usage. But if one wants to, one can further extend node.js by writing what is known as native modules. node.js provides a way of wrapping C++ code around JavaScript API and thus extending the V8 runtime just as core modules of node.js like fs and http does. There might be other reasons to create C++ modules. For example, to use legacy code or to gain performance. One can publish and distribute these packages just like usual node modules, the default entry point for a native module is `index.node` file. Writing native modules requires knowledge of a number of C++ libraries. We won't be discussing native modules in this book, that is much beyond the scope but worth mentioning.

Importing folders

Libraries hardly fit into a single file. The code for the simplest of libraries spans at least a few files. It makes sense to keep logically separate pieces of code in separate files, that is the whole point of modularization, and using `require` in the first place. Imagine you had to code your complete library, which is around 1000 lines of JavaScript code in a single file. How awful would that be? Let's turn that awful into awesome.

If node.js is unable to find the file with the specified name/path, node will look for a directory with the same name. On finding a directory with that exact name, the node, by default will try to load `index.js` file from the root of that directory. We can override that default but, this file should be the entry point into our library and because of the way node `require` works, it should be the single entry point.

So for our `simplemath` library, we shall have the following folder structure:

```
-simplemath
    index.js
    tests.js
        -lib
            sum.js
            subtract.js
            multiply.js
            divide.js
            constants.js
```

require cache

Whenever a file or module is required, the result obtained is cached. Subsequent `require` calls to the same file/module will serve the results from the cache. Let's enquire upon it. From the `simplemath` folder:

```
$ cd simplemath
$ node
> var sm = require("./index.js")
```

We have loaded the object in a variable named sm. Let's inspect the `require` object:

```
$ require
{ [Function: require]
  resolve: [Function],
  main: undefined,
  extensions:
   { '.js': [Function],
     '.json': [Function],
     '.node': [Function] },
```

```
    registerExtension: [Function],
    cache:
     { '/home/juzer/simplemath/index.js':
        { id: '/home/juzer/simplemath/index.js',
          exports: [Object],
          parent: [Object],
          filename: '/home/juzer/simplemath/index.js',
          loaded: true,
          children: [Object],
          paths: [Object] },
   ...
}
```

Check out the object, especially the cache property. It lists all the files that were required across our library and its dependencies. This object itself is the cache. Let's try to retrieve the function sum from the cache:

```
> var sum = require.cache["/home/juzer/simplemath/lib/sum.js"].exports
> sum
[Function]
sum(1,3)
4
```

Hence we could retrieve the sum function from the cache. In general a cached file can be retrieved from following reference:

```
require.cache["absolute-file-path"].exports
```

On each subsequent require, the import will be served from this location. Assigning some other value to the exports property will return that value instead. Hacking with the cache object can introduce weird bugs in your program. It's good to stay away from this for the most part.

One implication of caching is that the code inside a file is run only once. So you should make sure your .js files are not having any side effects. For example, incrementing a counter in the database to keep track of number of times a module was required or loaded in your code is not a good idea.

Another implication is that the same object is returned each time a require on a file or module is called. It's not a copy of the object, it is the same object. Hope you haven't closed your REPL yet. After performing the previous commands do the following:

```
$ sm.x = "some value..."
$ sm
{ PI: 3.141592653589793,
```

```
  E: 2.718281828459045,
  sum: [Function],
  subtract: [Function],
  multiply: [Function],
  divide: [Function],
  gcd: [Function: gcd],
 x: 'some value...' }
$ var sm2 = require("./index")
$sm2
{ PI: 3.141592653589793,
  E: 2.718281828459045,
  sum: [Function],
  subtract: [Function],
  multiply: [Function],
  divide: [Function],
  gcd: [Function: gcd],
  x: 'some value...' }
```

The x property in both the cases proves that, using the `require` function on the module two times, returned the same object.

Step 2 – writing tests

In `tests.js` add the following code, which tests the API of our library:

```
/* assert is used frequently during testing.  assert.equal checks if
   the two arguments passed to it are equal,  If they aren't, an error is
   immediately thrown.
   */
var assert = require("assert");

//index.js is the entrypoint into our library
var simplemath = require("./index");

assert.equal(simplemath.sum(1,2), 3);


assert.equal(simplemath.subtract(10, 6), 4);


assert.equal(simplemath.multiply(3, 5), 15);
```

```
    assert.equal(simplemath.divide(33, 3),11);


    assert.equal(simplemath.PI,3.141592653589793);

    console.info("All tests passed successfully!");
```

Running this test will of course result in us staring at a very ugly stack trace:

```
$ node tests.js
/home/juzer/Desktop/Instant NPM Handbook/simplemath/tests.js:4
assert(math.sum(1,2) === 3);
            ^

TypeError: Object #<Object> has no method 'sum'
    at Object.<anonymous> (/home/juzer/Desktop/Instant NPM Handbook/
simplemath/tests.js:4:13)
    at Module._compile (module.js:456:26)
    at Object.Module._extensions..js (module.js:474:10)
    at Module.load (module.js:356:32)
    at Function.Module._load (module.js:312:12)
    at Module.runMain (module.js:497:10)
    at process._tickCallback (node.js:427:13)
```

Calling math.sum failed because we still haven't written any code and calling require on an empty file will result in an empty object being assigned to simplemath variable. We will fix these errors one by one.

Step 3 – writing the actual code

Let's write the actual business logic that our module promises to solve. Let's add subtract, multiply, divide functions, and constants objects to our library.

Add the following code in the files mentioned:

simplemath/lib/subtract.js

```
    module.exports = function(num1, num2) {
            return num1 - num2;
            };
```

simplemath/lib/multiply.js

```
    module.exports = function(num1, num2) {
            return num1 * num2;
        };
```

simplemath/lib/divide.js

```
module.exports = function(num, denom) {
        return num / denom;
      };
```

simplemath/lib/constants.js

```
module.exports =  {
        E: Math.E,
        PI: Math.PI
      };
```

The functions subtracts, multiplies, and divides the provided arguments respectively. The constants.js file provides constants like PI and E borrowed directly from the in-built math library. It is an overkill to create a separate file for each function. In a typical scenario, we would put the complete simplemath code in a single file. Imagine if simplemath was a huge library and each of the functions were large components, then we could've probably justified splitting it in multiple files. For the sake of simplicity and illustration we have chosen to make ourselves believe that each function is really a large separate component.

Similarly, it is unnecessary to assign constants provided by the math library into our own object like we did in constants.js. We can just use the math library directly. But for illustrating how we can export objects, we chose the preceding example.

Step 4 – writing the glue code

Now let's look at simplemath/index.js and see how we can glue the different components together. As a best practice, this file should only contain glue code and not any logic.

simplemath/index.js

```
    // Attach all the components
  var simplemath = require("./lib/constants.js");
  simplemath.sum = require("./lib/sum.js");
  simplemath.subtract = require("./lib/subtract.js");
  simplemath.multiply = require("./lib/multiply");
  simplemath.divide = require("./lib/divide.js");

  //Expose the simplemath object and provide the entrypoint
  module.exports = simplemath;
```

Now let's run the test cases again:

```
$ node tests.js
```

All test cases passed successfully!

So here is our simplemath library. The code is modularized into different files and yet we are able to obtain a single object that exposes the complete API.

Step 5 – creating package.json

Every project has lots of metadata associated with it. For example, the name of the module, name of the author, links to official repository and issue tracking, dependencies, license, and so on. In a node module, all that information is stored inside `package.json` file. The `package.json` file lives in the root of the package folder.

Let us try to create a relevant `package.json` file for our library. npm is of great help here. The npm `init` command interactively creates `package.json` file for the project, with providing convenient defaults.

```
$ npm init
This utility will walk you through creating a package.json file. It only
covers the most common items, and tries to guess sane defaults.

See npm help json for definitive documentation on these fields and
exactly what they do.

Use npm install <pkg> --save afterwards, to install a package and save it
as a dependency in the package.json file.


Press ^C at any time, to quit.

name: (simplemath)
```

npm has started collecting information regarding the package. The first piece of information it is asking for is the package name. Note that it is important, this is the name by which our package will be found and identified on registry. npm has already suggested the name based on our folder name. Just hit the return key.

```
version: (0.0.0) 0.0.1
```

Next npm asks for version. This field too is important, npm keeps all the versions of a package and serves the requested package. Although npm is suggesting 0.0.0, but we have a working package so we will version it 0.0.1. After clicking on the *Enter* key.

```
description:
```

This is optional. npm is asking for a description of our package. Although it isn't required, it is a good practice to drop a one line description, for example, a simple math library.

```
entry point: (index.js)
```

Npm is asking for an entry point to our application. As we already know `index.js` is the default, but this is where we can override the default setting. Right now we shall go ahead with the default.

```
test command: node tests.js
```

This too is optional, npm is asking for a command that will run our tests. Putting `node tests.js` there, we will be able to run our tests by issuing the command npm test on command line.

`git repository:`

Open source projects are usually hosted on github or some other hosting provider. Here we can specify the git URL of our project. For now, we will skip it. Hit return without typing anything.

`keywords: math mathematics simple`

Whatever keywords we provide will be indexed by npm so that our package can be searched by those keywords. Give a space-separated list of words.

`author: yourname <yourname@email.com>`

Enter the name of the author, that is, your name, and optionally, e-mail ID in the given format.

`license: (BSD)`

Enter the license under which you want to publish your code. The default BSD is a good copyleft license that places very little restrictions upon users and promotes the spirit of open source.

`About to write to ~/simplemath/package.json:`

```
{
  "name": "simplemath",
  "version": "0.0.1",
  "description": "A simple math library",
  "main": "index.js",
  "devDependencies": {},
  "scripts": {
    "test": "test"
  },
  "repository": "",
  "keywords": [
    "math",
    "mathematics",
    "simple"
  ],
  "author": "yourname <yourname@email.com>",
  "license": "BSD"
}


Is this ok? (yes)
```

So here is our first `package.json` carrying precious information about our project. Hit enter, and hooray! A `package.json` file appears in our project root with the above contents written in it. npm will warn you that there is no `README.md` file in our package. It is a good practice to include a `README` file with detailed description of the package. If you want, include such a file in project root, but it is not required.

`Simplemath/README.md`

```
simplemath
=======
A simple math library
```

This is the most basic `package.json` file for a project; specifying name, description, version, and author name of the project. There is a lot more that `package.json` can do to share project related information with npm and automate repetitive tasks.

Step 6 – adding dependencies

We suddenly realize that for our purposes, we will also need a function in our `simplemath` library that calculates **greatest common divisor (gcd)** of two numbers. It will take some effort to write a well-tested `gcd` function, why not look around to see if someone has already implemented it. Go to `https://npmjs.org` and search for `gcd`. You will get scores of results. You may find lots of node modules solving the same problem. It is often difficult to choose between seemingly identical node modules. In such situations, check out the credentials of the developer(s) who are maintaining the project. Compare the number of times each module was downloaded by users. You can get this information on the package's page on npmjs at `https://npmjs.org/package/<pkg-name>`.

You can also check out the repository where the project is hosted, or the home page of the project. You will get this information on the npmjs home page of the module. If it isn't available, this probably isn't the module you want to use. If, however, it is available, check out the number of people who have starred the project on github, the number of people who have forked it, and active developers contributing to the project. Perhaps check out and run the test cases, or dive into the source code.

If you are betting heavily on a node module which isn't actively maintained by reputed developers, or which isn't well tested, you might be setting yourself up for a major rework in the future.

While we search for the gcd keyword on npmjs website we come to know that there is a node module named `mathutils` (`https://npmjs.org/package/mathutils`) that provides an implementation of `gcd`. We don't want to write our own implementation especially after knowing that someone somewhere in the node community has already solved that problem and published the JavaScript code. Now we want to be able to reuse that code from within our library.

Note that this use case is a little contrived and it is an overkill to include an external library for such simple tasks as to calculate GCD, which is as a matter of fact, very few lines of code, and is popular enough to be found easily. It is used here for the purpose of illustration.

We can do so very easily. Again npm command line will help us reduce the number of steps.

```
$npm install mathutils --save
```

We have asked npm to install `mathutils` and the `--save` flag, in the end saves it as a dependency in our `package.json` file. So the `mathutils` library is downloaded in `node_modules` folder inside our project. Our new `package.json` file looks like this.

```
{
    "name": "simplemath",
    "version": "0.0.1",
    "description": "A simple math library",
    "main": "index.js",
    "dependencies": {
      "mathutils": "0.0.1"
    },
    "devDependencies": {},
    "scripts": {
      "test": "test"
    },
    "repository": "",
    "keywords": [
      "math",
      "mathematics",
      "simple"
    ],
    "author": "yourname <yourname@email.com>",
    "license": "BSD"
}
```

And thus, `mathutils` is ready for us to use it as we please. Let's proceed to make use of it in our library.

1. Add the test case: Add the following code to test `gcd` function to the end of `tests.js` file but before `console.info`.

    ```
    assert.equal( simplemath.gcd(12, 8), 4 );
    console.log("GCD works correctly");
    ```

2. Glue the gcd function from mathutils to simplemath in index.js.

```
var mathutils = require("mathutils"); to load mathutils?
var simplemath = require("./lib/constants.js");

simplemath.sum = require("./lib/sum.js");
simplemath.subtract = require("./lib/subtract .js");
simplemath.multiply = require("./lib/multiply.js");
simplemath.divide = require("./lib/divide.js");
simplemath.gcd = mathutils.gcd;            // Assign gcd

module.exports = simplemath;
```

We have imported the mathutil library in our index.js and assigned the gcd function from the mathutil library to simplemath property with the same name. Let's test it out. Since our package.json is aware of the test script, we can delegate it to npm.

$ npm test

...

All tests passed successfully

Thus we have successfully added a dependency to our project.

The node_modules folder

We do not want to litter our node.js application directory with code from external libraries or packages that we want to use, npm provides a way of keeping our application code and third party libraries or node modules into separate directories. That is why the node_modules folder. Code for any third-party modules will go into this folder. From node.js documentation (http://nodejs.org/api/modules.html):

> If the module identifier passed to require() is not a native module, and does not begin with '/', '../', or './', then node starts at the parent directory of the current module, and adds /node_modules, and attempts to load the module from that location.

> If it is not found there, then it moves to the parent directory, and so on, until the root of the tree is reached.

> For example, if the file at '/home/ry/projects/foo.js' called require ('bar.js'), then node would look in the following locations, in this order:

✦ /home/ry/projects/node_modules/bar.js

✦ /home/ry/node_modules/bar.js

✦ /home/node_modules/bar.js

✦ /node_modules/bar.js

> This allows programs to localize their dependencies, so that they do not clash.

Whenever we run the npm install command, the packages get stored into the `node_modules` folder inside the directory in which the command was issued.

Each module might have its own set of dependencies, which are then installed inside `node_ modules` folder of that module. So in effect we obtain a dependency tree with each module having its dependencies installed in its own folder. Imagine two modules, on which your code is dependent, uses a different version of a third module. Having dependencies installed in their own folders, and the fact that `require` will look into the innermost `node_modules` folder first, affords a kind of safety that very few platforms are able to provide. Each module can have its own version of the same dependency. Thus node.js tactfully avoids dependency-hell which most of its peers haven't been able to do so far.

Step 7 – publishing

We have finished creating the simplemath node module Version 0.0.1 (denoted as simplemath@0.0.1) and we feel quite accomplished with it. Next thing is, we want to share it with the world. We want to make it available to anyone who could benefit from it, just as we could easily obtain and use `mathutils` package. Our package should be downloadable by anyone with a valid node.js installation by issuing `npm install simplemath` command.

Register and login

If this is the first time you are publishing a package, you will need to register yourself on the npm registry first. Here too, npm command line will be of great help to us. Whether or not you are already registered on npmjs, the steps to login through command line is pretty much the same.

```
$ npm login
Username:
```

If you are already logged in or if you have logged into npm from your computer before, npm may suggest the username. Choose a unique username for yourself.

```
Password:
```

Enter a password and be sure about it, because the command-line utility doesn't ask you to confirm the password.

```
Email:
```

Enter your e-mail ID and hit return. If everything went well you will see the following logs on your console.

```
npm http PUT https://registry.npmjs.org/-
\/user/org.couchdb.user:username

npm http 201 https://registry.npmjs.org/-
\/user/org.couchdb.user:username
```

Npm just called a REST APIs provided by the npm registry and registered you as a user. You can login with the same credentials on `https://npmjs.org/login`. If you are already a registered user you will see a slightly different log. Anyhow you should be successfully logged into the npm registry through npm command-line. Just make sure by doing the following:

```
$ npm whoami
```

And you should see your username printed on the console. Finally, lets proceed to publish our code

Publish

Before proceeding to publish our module I want to share a word of caution. npm registry is a free service that hosts node modules and thousands of developers use it. Namespace is a big problem on npmjs. Only one node module can be published under a name. It is not helpful to publish packages that will not be useful to a fair number of developers. It is just wasting away the namespace. We would rather see the `simplemath` namespace to be taken by some library that can provide non-trivial code to the users.

Although we will publish our package to learn the process, we will make sure that we don't take up a namespace that could accommodate a more robust package with which some non-trivial programs could be built. So rename your package such that it indicates that this is a trivial module. In `package.json` precede the package name with `x-` followed by your username and a hyphen. So it should look like this

```
{
   name: x-username-simplemath
   ...
}
```

now issue npm publish from inside the `simplemath` folder.

```
$ npm publish
npm http PUT https://registry.npmjs.org/x-username-simplemath
npm http 201 https://registry.npmjs.org/x-username-simplemath
npm http GET https://registry.npmjs.org/x-username-simplemath
npm http 200 https://registry.npmjs.org/x-username-simplemath
npm http PUT https://registry.npmjs.org/x-username-simplemath/0.0.1/-
\tag/latest
npm http 201 https://registry.npmjs.org/x-username-simplemath/0.0.1/-
\tag/latest
npm http GET https://registry.npmjs.org/x-username-simplemath
npm http 200 https://registry.npmjs.org/x-username-simplemath
```

```
npm http PUT https://registry.npmjs.org/x-username-simplemath/-/x-
username-simplemath-0.0.1.tgz/-rev/2-0c70b5d837c74d36d4e568b803c2896f
```

```
npm http 201 https://registry.npmjs.org/x-username-simplemath/-/x-
username-simplemath-0.0.1.tgz/-rev/2-0c70b5d837c74d36d4e568b803c2896f
```

```
+ x-username-simplemath@0.0.1
```

You have successfully published your first node module. To test it, go to a random folder in your computer, or on a different computer altogether, which has a valid node.js installation and run:

```
$ npm install x-username-simplemath
```

And you shall see your module get downloaded in `node_modules` folder in that directory.

Now, since we know that our package is not of use to many developers, we shall unpublish the module.

```
$ npm unpublish x-username-simplemath
```

```
...
```

```
- x-username-simplemath
```

And that completes our node module development flow.

Top 10 features you need to know about

We created and published our very first node module in the previous section. In this section we will learn tips and tricks to use features provided by npm to our advantage. The npm command-line utility offers a range of functionalities to help smoothen the development and deployment of node modules. Let's find out how can we exploit them. Here are the 10 things you should know.

Before we proceed, remember the glossary term prefix.

Prefix: {prefix} is the full path where node.js installation is kept on the system. On most of the systems, this is /usr/local. On Windows systems it is usually C:/Users/Username . So wherever you see the word prefix inside curly braces, think of this definition.

Tag

As we know that npm keeps multiple versions of a node module, we can associate a tag, which is a short name, to a particular version. For example, many popular node modules usually keep their latest stable version under a stable tag. npm automatically tags the most recent version of a node module as latest. Command for tagging is:

```
$ npm tag <package-name>@<version> [tag]
```

Remember we are tagging a specific version of a package with the tag name so specifying both package-name and version are mandatory. The specified version should have been published before tagging it on npm registry. Providing a tag name is optional, if not, present the npm defaults to latest.

Install

We have already seen npm install in action in the previous section. Let's revisit this command and see what we missed.

```
$ npm install
```

From inside a module directory which contains a valid `package.json`, installs all the packages listed as `dependencies` and `devDependencies` inside `package.json`, into the `./node_modules` folder. If no `package.json` exists at current path, npm will exit with an error. The version of the package that will be installed, depends on as specified in `package.json`. The dependency package's names are specified as keys of `dependencies`, `devDependencies`, and `optionalDependencies` property and their values indicate version. The version follows semver semantics. * means latest available version. Some more are:

+ \> or >=, that is, greater than or greater than or equal to the specified version

+ \< or <=, less than or less than or equal to the specified version

+ A version range, for example, >=0.5 <=1.0

+ An exact version string, for example, 1.2.3-beta.

Take a look at the sample `package.json`:

```
{...
  name: "pacakgename",
  "version": "0.0.1",
  dependencies: {
    "oauth": "0.9.8",
    "express": "*",
    "mongoskin": ">=0.2.0",
    "lodash": "< 1.0.0-rc.3",
    "passport": ">0.1.0 <=0.1.15"
    ...
  }
  ...
}
```

In this project, exact Version 0.9.8 of the `oauth` package will be installed. Latest available express package will be installed. Latest `mongoskin` available after 0.2.0 (inclusive) will be installed. Lodash Version less than 1.0.0-rc.3 will be installed. Any passport version available between 0.1.0 (not including 0.1.0 itself) and 0.1.15 (inclusive) will be installed with recent version taking precedence over earlier versions.

To understand **semver (semantic versioning)** semantics, that is exactly how package versions are sorted or which version pattern is considered recent than another, checkout `http://semver.org/` and `https://npmjs.org/doc/semver.html`.

Note: npm version semantics differ slightly from semver:

```
$ npm install <folder | tarball-file | tarball-url>
```

Pass to the argument either a folder name or a tarball name on filesystem containing a valid node module or a URL that serves such a tarball. This and subsequent commands accepts space separated list of dependencies to install in any combination:

```
$ npm install <package-name> [--save, --save-dev, --save-optional]
```

Looks up the latest version of `<package-name>` in the npm registry and installs it into the local `node_modules` directory.

Optionally provide `--save`, `--save-dev`, `--save-optional` switches to automatically update corresponding section in `package.json`. These switches are valid for subsequent install commands mentioned. `devDependencies` are dependencies which are required during development of the module but not while using it in production, for example, a testing framework, or assertion library which are required during development but are never used while actually running the code in production.

An `optionalDependency` is one without which a module should be able to run successfully. For example, the `redis` module comes with `hiredis` specified as an optional dependency. The `hiredis` module is a native module written in C++ that parses response from the redis server. If somehow `hiredis` could not be installed, redis uses JavaScript parser instead. So the `redis` module is able to function properly even without its optional dependency.

```
$ npm install <package-name>@<version | tag | version-range>
```

The preceding command installs the package with a given version number, tag, or version range. You can also specify version ranges, for example, `$ npm install mocha@">0.2.0 <=0.3.0"`. As discussed previously, they will be resolved according to semver semantics.

```
$ npm install <git-url>
```

For users who use git for version control, which is very likely since most node.js developers use git, you can directly install a package by cloning its git repository. By default, latest commit to master branch is fetched. You can specify a particular commit hashtag or git tag by appending `#<commit-hashtag | git-tag>` in the URL. One reason you would want to use a git URL directly is when the code is not published on npm, for example, when it is not an open source module and is not available on npm registry. Although you can have your own private npm registry, that will come at a cost of some technical overhead. This is the simplest way of obtaining private code at the moment. The downside of using a git URL directly is that you lose semver versioning, and installation is usually slower than installing from npm repository directly. While using a git URL, it is advisable to use a tag rather than simply a git URL, as it gives some control over the code that comes in. If you simply save a git URL in your `package.json`, whatever committed latest to the branch specified (master by default) will be installed and that could be something broken. Tags are usually stable releases, which can be relied upon.

Related commands

The next command is issued from inside a project. It updates all the dependencies inside the project to the latest. Providing a list of package names or unique identifiers, it only updates those packages. Provide a --global or -g flag to update globally installed packages:

```
$ npm update [pkg...]
```

The next command uninstalls all the packages, list of package names, or package identifiers, provided:

```
$ npm uninstall [pkg..]
```

Binaries and global installs

A lot of software programs provide a command-line interface to use them. For example, npm itself is an excellent command-line program. Similarly, express and tower.js provide command-line helpers that create scaffoldings for web applications. The files containing the programs that run on a command from the command line are loosely referred to as binaries or executables.

To use binaries provided by external modules, express, for example, install them globally. Any package can be installed from npm registry globally by passing --global or -g command-line flag to the install command. For example:

```
$ npm install -g express
```

The previous command installs express globally. The executable will be available on the command line.

```
$ express myapp
```

The previous command will create a new folder myapp and create express scaffold for a minimal express web application.

To include an executable in a node module, it is required to include a file that can parse the command-line arguments and provide a command-line entry point to the application. The binary will probably call the programmatic API of the node module.

It is required to register the binary entry point in package.json. Take a look at express's reduced package.json.

```
{
    "name": "express",
    "description": "Sinatra inspired web development framework",
    "version": "3.0.1",
    ...
    "bin": { "express": "./bin/express" },
    ...
}
```

The `package.json` tells us that express keeps its binary in `express/bin` folder with the name express and if we care to look inside express's directory structure we will find that to be the case. Let's try to create a binary ourselves. Let's extend our `simplemath` library and provide a command-line API for just adding two numbers.

```
$ simplemath-add 2 3
5
```

First make `package.json` aware of a binary:

```json
{
    "name": "simplemath",
    "version": "0.0.1",
    "description": "A simple math library",
    "main": "index.js",
    "dependencies": {
        "mathutils": "~0.0.1"
    },
    "devDependencies": {},
    "scripts": {
        "test": "node tests.js"
    },
    "repository": "",
    "keywords": [
        "math",
        "mathematics",
        "simple"
    ],
    "bin": {"simplemath-add": "./bin/simplemath"},
    "author": "yourname <yourname@email.com>",
    "license": "BSD"
}
```

The highlighted code in the preceding code snippet, as we will see, will expose the `./bin/simplemath-add` file (binary) to the command line from the system's binary folder.

Now add a file `./bin/simplemath-add` to the project with the following contents.

```javascript
#!/usr/bin/env node

var simplemath = require("../index");        //Obtain simplemath object
var result;

// Parse the 2nd and 3rd arguments into integer values since that
iswhat our
```

```
// program expects. Preceding an evaluation with "+" sign is a
shorthand method
// of parsing the evaluation to a number.
var num1 = +process.argv[3];
var num2 = +process.argv[4];

// Do the math and print result
result = simplemath.sum(num1, num2);
console.log( result );
```

The first line in the previous program is called a shebang. In *nix environments, it is used to inform the command line to treat the rest of the file as binary of the given program. We tell it to treat our file as a node.js binary. Let us run the program and see. First provide execute permission to the file if you are on a *nix machine:

```
$ chmod u+x ./bin/simplemath-add
```

```
$ ./bin/simplemath-add sum 4 5
```

```
9
```

And it works perfectly well. But wait, why do we need to give the full path of our binary? We want to be able to access the command-line API globally, from any folder, without needing to type the full path. We need to install our package globally. After we publish this code to npm registry and then install `simplemath` from registry with a `--global` or simply `-g` flag, we will be able to do so. You can try it if you want.

You do not necessarily have to publish and install/update your package globally from npm registry, there is another way to do this in development environment. That is through linking, which is our next topic.

Related commands

The next command shows the folder in which globally installed module's binaries are kept:

```
$ npm --global bin
```

The next command will show path to binaries kept inside a local install:

```
$ npm bin
```

The next command updates all globally installed packages. If a list of package names or identifiers are mentioned, updates only them:

```
$ npm update --global [pkg...]
```

The next command uninstalls a globally installed package:

```
$ npm uninstall --global pkg
```

Linking

Often you want to use the latest, bleeding edge version of your node module, or someone else's module, which hasn't been published yet. One option is to keep the latest project folder into `node_modules` folder of another project. But that can quickly become taxing with deeply nested dependencies, or impossible to maintain if the node module is a circular dependency. Also imagine a case where we want to use the bleeding edge version of our node module in three different projects. Every time we make changes to our module, we will have to copy paste it in all three. npm has a better solution:

```
npm link
```

```
npm link <package-name>
```

Linking allows you to bootstrap a project as a dependency in another, so that the changes in one immediately can be used or tested in the other. To understand this let us again take the example of our simplemath node module. Imagine we are building another node module called advancedmath, that internally uses simplemath as a dependency. Perhaps we are building both modules simultaneously and we always want to use the latest version of `simplemath` in advancedmath.

So `advancedmath` will perhaps, have following folder structure:

```
- advancedmath
  + lib
     pacakge.json
     index.json
  - node_modules
  + simplemath
```

`package.json` of `advancedmath` should look like the following code snippet:

```
{
  "name": "advancedmath",
  "version": "0.0.0",
  "dependencies": {
    "simplemath": "*"
  }
}
```

As we have already discussed, we won't simply keep `simplemath` folder inside `advancedmath/node_modules` folder. There are better ways to keep ourselves sane. We will link the `simplemath` into `advancedmath`. You will require admin privileges on the computer, to do this, refer to the following commands:

```
$ cd path/to/simplemath
```

```
$ sudo npm link
```

The previous command links `simplemath` into a global installation and creates the simplemath binary that we have created in previous section, available globally. So we can do the following without publishing and installing our module globally from registry.

```
$ cd /some/random/folder
$ simplemath-add sum 1 3
4
```

Now let us bootstrap it to `advancedmath`, so that changes in `simplemath` are immediately reflected in `advancedmath` dependency of it.

```
$ cd path/to/advancedmath
$ npm link simplemath
```

The previous command has bootstrapped `simplemath` into `advancedmath`. It should be noted that any changes in binary would also affect the executable we are accessing from the command line.

If you are familiar with UNIX symlinks, it will probably interest you that a symlink to the globally installed `simplemath` folder is created inside `advancedmath/node_modules` directory. Hence any change is immediately reflected. Now we can independently develop the two modules without the `advancedmath` developer worrying about keeping abreast with `simplemath`, except for API changes of course. Notice that we didn't have to give the full path of `simplemath` while linking it inside `advancedmath` folder, although we may do so if we want, but the result will be same, `simplemath` will be installed globally before being linked to `advancedmath`.

Any folder installed globally, either by linking or by installing with `-g` flag can be linked to other projects as dependencies.

We can remove the bootstrapping anytime by executing `npm rm simplemath` or `npm uninstall simplemath` from inside `advancedmath` folder or by simply deleting the `simplemath` symlink from `advancedmath/node_modules`.

To remove global installation of the package, use the same command that is used to remove global installation of external packages.

```
$ npm uninstall -g simplemath
```

As seen in the previous section, linking also symlinks the binaries included in the module to the system's global binary folder. On the Linux environments those may be included in `/usr/bin`, `usr/sbin`, `/usr/local/bin`, `usr/local/sbin`, and so on.

Bear in mind that linking does not work on Windows without cygwin.

.npmignore

If you have used git and know what `.gitignore` does, `.npmignore` does pretty much the same thing. It is used to provide lists of files and folders to exclude while publishing the package. For example, our module might be generating a lot of log information in a log file while being tested. We don't want to include those in deployable builds since they are irrelevant to other users and unnecessarily increase package size.

We also might have some configuration files containing sensitive information like usernames and passwords. We don't want to have to remember every time we deploy to delete or move those files out of the folder before publishing the module. `.npmignore` is a newline delimited list of file names or patterns. The following patterns are recognized:

✦ `filename`: File or folder with this name anywhere in the module will not be included in the bundle. For example, we don't want to include test files in the production bundle so we can add `tests.js`. We also don't want to include the node_modules folder because we expect npm to install all the dependencies recursively for our module users, so we might also include node_modules.

✦ `*.ext`: File ending in .ext. For example *.log will ignore all files ending in .log and hence all of the log files.

✦ `folder/<filename>`: Ignore file only in particular folder.

✦ `folder/*.ext`: File ending in .ext in a particular folder.

✦ `folder/*`: All files inside a particular folder.

✦ `folder/**/filename`: any number of folders between folder and file.

✦ `directory/`: Only matches a directory named directory and not files named directory.

Remember, lines starting with hash (#) are treated as comments. To override that behavior, escape # with a backslash (\). For a comprehensive list of patterns visit `http://git-scm.com/docs/gitignore`. The page is for `.gitignore` but same rules applies to `.npmignore` as well.

A common `.npmignore` file has the following content:

```
node_modules/
npm-debug.log

# other patterns
```

The above two patterns are ignored by default during npm publishing and don't need to be mentioned in the `.npmignore` file explicitly.

Global .npmignore

A common npmignore for all packages for all the users can be defined at `{prefix}/etc/npmignore`. This default can be overridden by specifying a file path in **globalignoreconfig** configuration. To know more about npm configuration please see the *Config* section.

Scripts

npm allows you to run arbitrary scripts on certain events, for example, before a module gets downloaded, or before the module gets published. These scripts could be anything, for example, to clean up files or to clean up some system state. Following scripts are available from npm scripts official documentation:

- `prepublish`: Run before the package is published. (Also run on local npm install without any arguments.)
- `publish`, `postpublish`: Run after the package is published.
- `preinstall`: Run before the package is installed.
- `install`, `postinstall`: Run after the package is installed.
- `preuninstall`, `uninstall`: Run BEFORE the package is uninstalled.
- `postuninstall`: Run after the package is uninstalled.
- `preupdate`: Run before the package is updated with the update command.
- `update`, `postupdate`: Run after the package is updated with the update command.
- `pretest`, `test`, `posttest`: Run by the npm `test` command.
- `prestop`, `stop`, `poststop`: Run by the npm `stop` command.
- `prestart`, `start`, `poststart`: Run by the npm `start` command. If there is a `server.js` file present in the root of the package this command will default to `node server.js`.
- `prerestart`, `restart`, `postrestart`: Run by the npm `restart` command.

 npm restart will run the stop and start scripts if no restart script is provided.

`Test`, `start`, `stop`, and `restart` scripts are run when the commands are called directly from the command line. Remember we had delegated test scripts to npm in previous sections by providing `node tests.js` to `test` property of the `scripts` object inside our project's `package.json`. Similarly, we can provide scripts to be run through the command line for other events mentioned previously as well.

```
{...
  "scripts": {
      "update": "echo 'Updating'",
      "start": "echo 'starting'",
      "stop": "echo 'stopping'",
      "prepublish": "echo 'About to publish'",
      "postpublish": "echo 'Published already!'"
    },
  ...
}
```

An interesting bit to know is that these npm scripts are aware of binaries inside `./node_modules/.bin` even if they aren't installed globally.

Config

npm configuration are lists of key-value pairs comprising convenient defaults, information of user and computer, SSL certificates, and so on. For example, npm config stores the URL of standard registry; or npmjs username of a user who is currently logged in and its session information; or number of retries npm should make if a package installation fails for any reason. Let us check out what the registry URL is in npm config:

```
$ npm config get registry
https://registry.npmjs.org/
```

If the user wishes, he/she can change the default and provide a URL of a custom registry maintained by someone else or by themselves. The command for printing a config value on console is:

```
$ npm config get <key>
```

Or simply:

```
$ npm get <key>
```

Command for changing a config setting is:

```
$ npm config set <key> <value>
```

Or simply:

```
$ npm set <key> <value>
```

npm reads these values from a number of sources. The following are the sources from where npm picks up configs in the order of their precedence.

Command-line flag

Config information provided in the command line is of highest precedence. For example, to install a package from an alternate registry:

```
$ npm install <pacakge-identifier> --registry <registry-url>
```

The previous command doesn't persist the `config` value. To provide any config information in a command, include a flag with the config key followed by the value you want to set for that command: `--<key> <value>`.

Environment variables

Next, npm looks for a config value in the environment variable. The name of an environment variable corresponding to a config should be the config key preceded by `npm_config_`. So for example, to provide the configuration for loglevel in an environment variable, the variable should be named `npm_config_loglevel`.

User config file

Usually the file placed in `$HOME/.npmrc`, where `$HOME` is the logged-in user's home on the computer (`/home/username` on Unix, `C:/Users/Username` on Windows), or the userconfig configuration value set in either an environment variable or in the command line.

This file is an INI file, a formatted list of key-value pairs. We can use environment variables in this file by replacing with `${ENVIRONMENT_VARIABLE}`. So for example, to provide configuration for maximum number of retries, npm should make for installing a package, we would write following in the `config` file:

```
fetch-retries = 3
```

Global config file

Global config file is similar to user config file. But global config file is for all the users on the computer. This file should be placed at `{prefix}/etc/npmrc`.

Defaults

Defaults refer to the defaults from npm or node.js source. This is not meant to be changed by npm users but by distributors who maintain their own node.js or npm fork.

So these are the places from where npm reads the configuration. Following the command is to get a list of configs defined on a computer:

```
$ npm config list
```

Provide a `--long` or `-l` switch to get the full list. To edit the user config file, execute the following command:

```
$ npm config edit
```

This will open the user config file (`$HOME/.npmrc`) on the system's default text editor. On Linux this defaults to vi, for Windows, notepad is the default. To read man pages for config:

```
$ npm help config
```

Shrinkwrap

npm has this way of fetching the latest package available, according to the semver version-range we give it. Whether we are publishing our package to registry or using it internally within our organization, sometimes it is not a good idea to publish a module which will probably be used by many in production, with loosely packed dependencies. You might never know what hell might break loose with updates to any of your dependencies or your dependencies' dependencies and so on.

Sometimes it is useful to deploy a node.js application with dependencies locked to exact versions against which it was tested so that we can have predictable results in the end. Although we can manage to provide exact versions of each of our dependencies, we cannot expect the same from every author. Our dependencies and their dependencies might have dependencies loosely defined.

Shrinkwrap command, given it was run inside a valid npm package root, creates a file `npm-shrinkwrap.json` in the project root. It is a `.json` file similar to `package.json` except that its `dependencies` property recursively defines the exact version of each and every dependency that our project uses. The prerequisites of executing the shrinkwrap command are:

+ All the dependencies indicated in `package.json` should be installed, no packages should be missing

+ No extraneous packages, that is other than those mentioned in `package.json` dependencies should be installed

Pruning

npm prune removes all the extraneous packages, that is, those packages not mentioned in `package.json`.

Running `npm install` inside a project or a package with `npm-shrinkwrap.json` file will pick up dependency versions from the `npm-shrinkwrap.json` file instead of `package.json`.

To shrinkwrap a project, run the following command inside the project root.

```
$ npm shrinkwrap
wrote npm-shrinkwrap.json
```

You will find the mentioned file. Take a look at reduced `npm-shrinkwrap.json` obtained on running shrinkwrap on mocha.

```json
{
  "name": "mocha",
  "version": "1.8.1",
  "dependencies": {
```

```
    "commander": {
      "version": "0.6.1",
      "from": "commander@0.6.1"
    },
    "growl": {
      "version": "1.7.0",
      "from": "growl@1.7.x"
    },
    "jade": {
      "version": "0.26.3",
      "from": "jade@0.26.3",
      "dependencies": {
        "mkdirp": {
          "version": "0.3.0",
          "from": "mkdirp@0.3.0"
        }
      }
    },
// Other dependencies
```

Take a look at jade and its dependency `mkdirp`, the version of both the packages have recursively been locked down.

Run `npm ls` in a project root and see the how npm beautifully prints the dependency tree on the console. It even indicates if there are unmet or extraneous dependencies in the project.

Publishing

We used publish command in quick start, lets revisit and see what all things we can do with our packages on npm registry. Inside a project root `npm publish` publishes the node module. We can also do the following:

```
$ npm publish <folder | tarball>
```

From outside the project root, we can either specify the path to folder or the path to tarball or a URL to the tarball to publish. A new version should be mentioned in `package.json` every time we publish a module. Trying to publish a module with the same version twice will result in failure. But adding a `--force` flag will overwrite the version.

To unpublish a version use the following command:

```
$ npm unpublish <package-name>[@version]
```

The previous command removes the provided version of the package. To remove entire package and free the namespace on npm, drop the version part and provide `--force` flag.

 `npm pack` from inside a package root creates a tarball of the package without `node_modules` folder. Npm uses this command for creating a tarball to send to registry for publishing. It comes handy in inspecting the final contents that will go on npm publish. Check out other variants of pack command from man pages. `npm help pack`

And finally you can add/remove module owners to the packages that you own and that are published on registry.

To add an owner, follow the given command:

```
$ npm owner add <username> <packag-name>
```

In the previous command `<username>` is the username of the user registered on `http://npmjs.org` and `<package-name>` is the name of the published package owned by you. This command adds an owner, which has full rights to publish, upgrade, unpublish, or completely remove the package from npm. The added owner can even remove other owners, including the one who added him in the first place, so be careful with this command and add owners only that you completely trust. This might change, and npm suggests providing more fine-grained access control in future.

Similarly, to remove an owner use the following command:

```
$ npm owner rm <username> <packag-name>
```

And to list owners of a package use the following command:

```
$ npm owner ls <packag-name>
```

To run the previous command you don't need to be the owner of the mentioned package.

Help

Lastly, the best way to help yourself is to use help provided through npm man pages. Here are few commands to get quick help:

```
$ npm
```

Just running npm command provides a brief, non-exhaustive list of npm commands. Providing an `-1` switch will provide a more exhaustive list.

```
$ npm faq
```

The previous command opens man page for frequently asked npm questions.

```
$ npm <command> -h
```

The previous command provides quick help on the command.

```
$ npm help <term>
```

The previous command opens man page for the term and/or associated command, and gives a detailed description. For example, `npm help publish` or `npm help star`.

```
$ npm help npm
```

The previous command opens a detailed document of npm, its purpose and the way it works.

You can also text search through npm man pages using the `help-search` command.

```
$ npm help-search <text>
```

The `help-search` command will search for text and display the search results and their locations in man pages on command line.

People and places you should get to know

Knowing a technology also means knowing the community centered around it. Here is a compilation of twitter handles, websites, blogs of people and organizations, from where you can get the latest happenings in the world of node.js. You will also get a lot of inspiration and node.js best practices from these sources.

Official sites

+ Home page: `http://nodejs.org`
+ Manual and documentation: `http://nodejs.org/api`
+ Wiki: `https://github.com/joyent/node/wiki`
+ Blog: `http://blog.nodejs.org/`
+ Source code: `https://github.com/joyent/node`

Articles and tutorials

+ The node aesthetic: `http://substack.net/node_aesthetic`
+ Asynchronous control flow with promises: `http://howtonode.org/promises`
+ The philosophy behind node.js and what you should keep in mind while writing node modules:
  `http://blog.izs.me/post/48281998870/unix-philosophy-and-node-js`
+ This is how Substack writes modules: `http://substack.net/how_I_write_modules`
+ The place to get started with streams:
  `https://github.com/substack/stream-handbook`

Community

+ Official mailing list and forum: `http://groups.google.com/group/nodejs`
+ Official issue tracker: `https://github.com/joyent/node/issues`
+ Unofficial forums: `http://stackoverflow.com/questions/tagged/node.js`
+ Official IRC channel: #node.js on `irc.freenode.net`, and the web URL:
  `http://webchat.freenode.net/`
+ FAQ: `http://docs.nodejitsu.com/`

Blogs

✦ Nodejitsu team has node.js at the core of their PaaS, they often write about their challenges, failures, and successes with node: `http://blog.nodejitsu.com/`

✦ Isaac Schlueter is a core node.js contributor and is currently leading the node.js development. He is also the author of npm. This is the place where he blogs: `http://blog.izs.me`

✦ Substack has authored more than 100 node modules and he shares his experience, and philosophy on this blog: `http://substack.net/`

✦ Planet node.js compiles blogs from a number of sources and has rich content, `http://www.planetnodejs.com/`

✦ Strong loop very frequently spreads the news about what is happening in node.js world `http://blog.strongloop.com/`

Twitter

✦ Issac Schlueter: `https://twitter.com/izs`

✦ TJ Holowaychuk: `https://twitter.com/tjholowaychuk`

✦ Nathan Rajlich: `https://twitter.com/TooTallNate`

✦ Nuno Job: `https://twitter.com/dscape`

✦ James Halliday: `https://twitter.com/substack`

✦ Max Ogden: `https://twitter.com/maxogden`

✦ For more Open Source information, follow Packt at `http://twitter.com/#!/packtopensource`

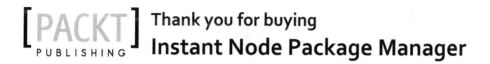

About Packt Publishing

Packt, pronounced 'packed', published its first book "*Mastering phpMyAdmin for Effective MySQL Management*" in April 2004 and subsequently continued to specialize in publishing highly focused books on specific technologies and solutions.

Our books and publications share the experiences of your fellow IT professionals in adapting and customizing today's systems, applications, and frameworks. Our solution based books give you the knowledge and power to customize the software and technologies you're using to get the job done. Packt books are more specific and less general than the IT books you have seen in the past. Our unique business model allows us to bring you more focused information, giving you more of what you need to know, and less of what you don't.

Packt is a modern, yet unique publishing company, which focuses on producing quality, cutting-edge books for communities of developers, administrators, and newbies alike. For more information, please visit our website: www.packtpub.com.

Writing for Packt

We welcome all inquiries from people who are interested in authoring. Book proposals should be sent to author@packtpub.com. If your book idea is still at an early stage and you would like to discuss it first before writing a formal book proposal, contact us; one of our commissioning editors will get in touch with you.

We're not just looking for published authors; if you have strong technical skills but no writing experience, our experienced editors can help you develop a writing career, or simply get some additional reward for your expertise.

CoffeeScript Programming with jQuery, Rails, and Node.js

ISBN: 978-1-84951-958-8   Paperback: 140 pages

Learn CoffeeScript programming with the three most popular web technologies around

1. Learn CoffeeScript, a small and elegant language that compiles to JavaScript and will make your life as a web developer better

2. Explore the syntax of the language and see how it improves and enhances JavaScript

3. Build three example applications in CoffeeScript step by step

SolarWinds Orion Network Performance Monitor

ISBN: 978-1-84968-848-2   Paperback: 336 pages

An essential guide for installing, implementing, and calibrating SolarWinds Orion PM

1. Master wireless monitoring and the control of wireless access points

2. Learn how to respond quickly and efficiently to network issues with SolarWinds Orion NPM

3. Build impressive reports to effectively visualize issues, solutions, and the overall health of your network

Please check **www.PacktPub.com** for information on our titles

Using Node.js for UI Testing

ISBN: 978-1-78216-052-6   Paperback: 146 pages

Learn how to easily automate testing of your web apps using Node.js, Zombie.js and Mocha

1. Use automated tests to keep your web app rock solid and bug-free while you code

2. Use a headless browser to quickly test your web application every time you make a small change to it

3. Use Mocha to describe and test the capabilities of your web app

Node Cookbook

ISBN: 978-1-84951-718-8   Paperback: 342 pages

Over 50 recippes to master the art of asynchronous server-side JavaScript using Node

1. Packed with practical recipes taking you from the basics to extending Node with your own modules

2. Create your own web server to see Node's features in action

3. Work with JSON, XML, web sockets, and make the most of asynchronous programming

Please check **www.PacktPub.com** for information on our titles

www.ingramcontent.com/pod-product-compliance
Lightning Source LLC
Chambersburg PA
CBHW060442060326
40690CB00019B/4303